musings
of a curious
aesthete

Leonard Koren

Drawings by Marco Koren

Imperfect Publishing

Point Reyes, California

For Emilia, Kitty, and Nell

Published by Imperfect Publishing
PO Box 608, Point Reyes, CA 94956 USA

Book design by Emilia Burchiellaro and the author.

Special thanks to Jonathan Braun, Gary Gach, Peter Goodman,
Yvonne Israel-O'Hare, Peter Levitt, Mariah Nielsen, Michael
Phillips, Marta Salas-Porras, and Kitty Whitman for their help
in the making of this book.

imperfectpublishing.com

Printed in Canada

ISBN 978-0981484679

contents

introduction

During an interview with a journalist from a shelter magazine, I was asked, "So, what's it like being an aesthete?"[1] I was taken aback. I took the question as a veiled criticism, not as a compliment. Aesthetes, I thought, were vain, pompous, self-absorbed creatures obsessively preoccupied with beauty. Is that how I came across? More importantly, is that what I was? ✳ After pondering that question for a few months, I concluded that yes, I probably was an aesthete, at least in part. I have always been drawn to beauty. Understanding beauty was the basis of my life's work. By beauty I mean the highest aesthetic good. It was in beauty that I found an almost inexhaustible source of pleasure and meaning. And it was in beauty that I discovered a world that finally made sense. (Well, sort of.)

+ + +

This is a book about aesthetics from the point of view of an aesthete. It is anecdotal rather than scholarly. That is, it is a recounting of personal experiences and thoughts rather than a rehashing of ideas I studied in an academic sense or acquired through reading.

"Aesthetics" is a slippery term. It is so vexing that I once attempted to pin it down. I focused on the ten or so ways that I routinely used it. I found the following definition, in spite of its clunkiness, to be the most generally useful for the purposes of my work:

- "Aesthetics" is all about a *cognitive mode* in which you are aware of, and think about, the sensory and emotive qualities of phenomena and things.

- It is the "thinking about" that distinguishes the aesthetic from the merely sensorial or hedonistic.

- "Sensorial" means not only the sensations of touch, taste, smell, sight, and sound, but also cerebral "feelings"—like the tingle of evocative ideas coursing through your brain.

- Sensory and emotive qualities can be abstract, like the overall tone or feeling of a culture. Or they can be very particular, like the poetic resonance of a name given to a type of subatomic particle. (*Quark! Quark!*)

- No one particular type of object or phenomenon is more or less suited than another to be a catalyst for, or the subject of, aesthetic experience.

- In the aggregate, virtually all of what we refer to as "reality" is an essentially aesthetic experience. Everything we know about the world, except what is genetically encoded, comes to us through our senses and is then intellectually, emotionally, or otherwise processed.[2]

+ + +

This volume is divided into two sections. "Nostalgia," the first part, is an account of how I became "me." "Me" is, of course, the person who wrote these words. "Me" is also a universal archetype. "Me" is every creator who yearns, learns, expends energy, and engages their will to make things that aspire to the beautiful— however one understands "beautiful."

"Criticism," the second part, is an overview of some of the things that I have been thinking about lately.

nostalgia

beauty v. ugliness

For most of my adult life I have generated ideas intended to help other artists, designers, and creators in their work. I called these ideas "conceptual tools." I packaged these conceptual tools as theories, paradigms, vocabularies, taxonomies, narratives, and critical perspectives. I disseminated them through books that I wrote, designed, and often published.

Once a book is published it can never be unpublished. This is why I have aborted about as many book projects as I have brought to fruition. If a book failed to offer up some new and compelling conceptual tool/s, I didn't think it was worth publishing. On a few occasions, however, I overrode this policy.

+ + +

"A rhetoric of object placement" is how I described one of the conceptual tools I developed. I took the elements of rhetoric—the Ancient Greek civic art of persuasive verbal communication—and refashioned them into a system for creating more effective visual presentations. My intended audience was photo stylists, window-display designers, interior decorators, etc. In other words, people who make a living arranging objects to engage the observer in an aesthetic response.

Much of the research for this project was conducted in Europe.[3] On my last day in Vienna a store, if indeed it was a store, caught my eye. Looking through its front window I glimpsed an unusually refined and elegant environment. It didn't fit into any of the commercial typologies I was familiar with. It was a Sunday and the business was closed—as was everything else on the block. I had many questions, but there was no one around to ask.

On a subsequent trip to Vienna I headed straight back to that enigmatic store. It turned out to be a flower shop. (When I had walked by the first time I hadn't seen any flowers.)[4] I was greeted by a pleasant young man, one of the four full-time staff members. A lively conversation ensued. He told me that he had once considered becoming either an artist or a social worker. Instead he studied the floral arts at a school in Germany whose curriculum was based on an esoteric naturalistic philosophy. After graduation he was invited to Japan to teach what he had learned. While there he had read one of my books.

+ + +

The flower shop occupied the ground floor of a stately nineteenth-century apartment building. Between the polished concrete floors and the twenty-two-foot-high ceilings there was an immense volume of what felt like "sacred space." A huge photograph of a motorcycle abandoned in a field of wildflowers graced one wall. Its purpose was to set the shop's aesthetic tone for that year. Facing the image was a life-sized stuffed giraffe guarding the entrance to the shop's tiny business office. (It was on loan from a local zoological institution.) Scattered everywhere were fresh flowers in vases of various sizes and shapes. The larger vases sat on the floor. The others were either atop pedestals of concrete and steel or arranged on the shelves of an ingenious freestanding display system. Flowers past their prime were gathered in a back area called the "flower hospice" where children, students—and anyone else—could take what they wanted for free. At the shop's center was a long, sleek, stainless-steel working table. I accidentally knocked it as I walked by. It began to wiggle (and wiggle, and wiggle . . .). I was told this was a charming design flaw that everyone had grown to love.

At the end of my brief visit I was still curious, so I asked the shop's owner if I could come back as an observer. Over the next year and a half I returned five more times for stays of from four days to three weeks. I took lots of notes, shot countless photographs, and conducted interviews with the staff, suppliers, and customers. Mostly, however, I simply watched and listened.

I was particularly enthralled by the client-staff interactions. Most of the clients were regulars, so various levels of intimacy had already been established. Flowers were selected as staff and clients wandered about the shop. Then, back at the wiggly table, the arranging commenced. From my perch on an old sofa near the back window, it was like watching theater: Flowers and other plant materials danced between dexterous hands as vivid expressions of joy, sadness, love, and tenderness coalesced. Beauty was in play. Beauty was at play. Euphoria hovered. Transcendence was palpable.

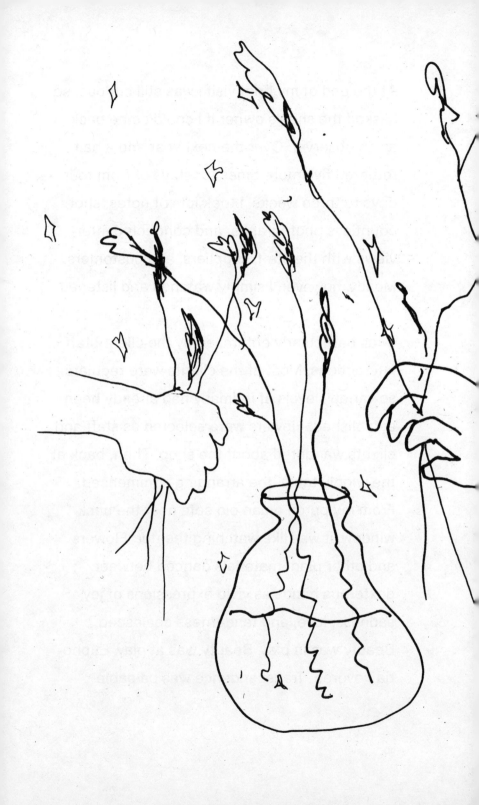

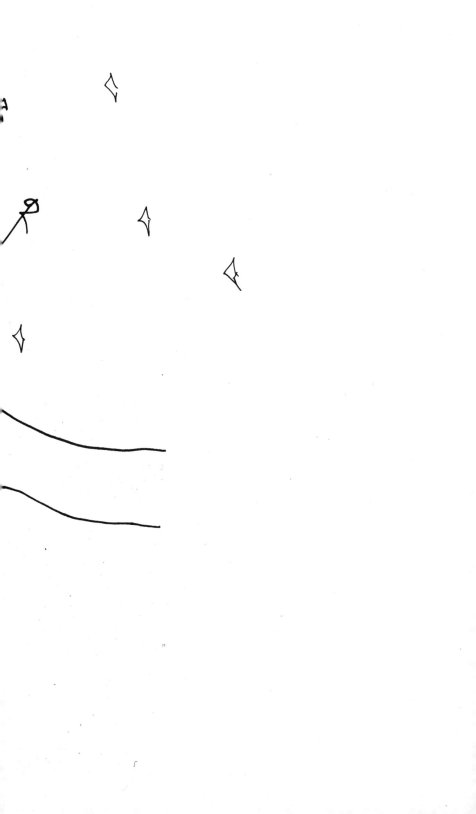

My plan was to distill this all down into a book-length paradigm to enable others to recreate the magic. But I had missed something. The genius of the shop was in its quintessential particularity. That is, the unique coming together of distinct personalities and creative visions in a historically idiosyncratic urban culture. When I finally understood the singularity of the situation—and thus the impossibility of what I was attempting—I realized that it was time to pull the plug, to terminate the project.

+ + +

A few weeks later I was in New York. Among other things, I was scheduled to have dinner with a professional acquaintance, an architectural designer and writer. At one point during our meal, he asked what my ethnicity was. I thought this an odd question, but answered anyway. Then, without a hint of irony or humor, he began demeaning this ethnicity. At first he was subtle, but soon he brought up long-discredited libels and wacky political conspiracy theories. He clearly had an agenda, though I couldn't fathom what it was. I tried to change the subject, but he wouldn't let it go. I was astonished but also upset. I was so upset that I said very little.

I didn't sleep well that night. The unpleasantness of the evening kept running through my brain. Someone I had assumed would be respectful and mindful of the feelings of others turned out to be otherwise. I was also troubled by my reluctance to mount a forceful response. Around three in the morning I got out of bed. Just before dawn I went striding through the city.

As my thoughts and feelings clarified, a desire to do something took hold. But what? How do you retroactively counter ugliness? With more ugliness? No. Then it struck me: I had just been with a group of beautifully behaved human beings in a beautiful environment in which beauty was being continuously generated. What about a documentary account of what went on in the flower shop? But such a book, bereft of any new or useful conceptual tools, would run afoul of one of my most cherished publishing principles. What to do? After running through my hierarchy of personal values, it became clear: I must neutralize the ugliness with the most formidable aesthetic good at my disposal. So I set to work on a book. The title of that book was *The Flower Shop: Charm, Grace, Beauty & Tenderness in a Commercial Context.*[5]

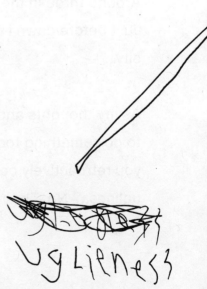

Beauty

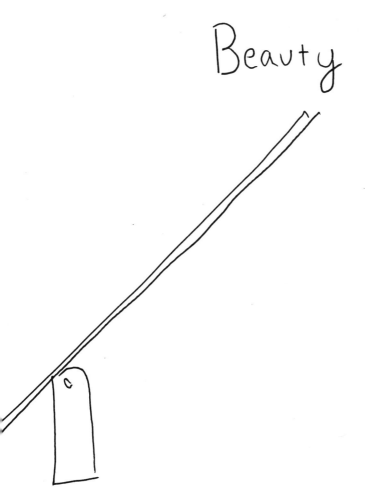

beginnings

Before I came into the world, my Brooklyn born-and-bred mother was a buyer for a fashionable Manhattan department store. I was still in diapers when she, my father, and I moved to Los Angeles. After finally settling in, my mother applied her intelligence and charm to social work. She never lost her strong opinions about beauty and taste though—which, for the most part, I absorbed. Periodically my mother rearranged the artworks throughout our home. I was often enlisted to help. She would hold up a framed drawing, painting, or print and ask me where it should be placed on a particular wall. I was always praised for my aesthetic judgments.

My father was born in Odessa, which was then part of Imperial Russia. At the conclusion of the Russian Revolution his family fled to Istanbul, then called Constantinople. When he was seventeen he emigrated to the United States with

his widowed mother and two siblings. He immediately went to work for an uncle who manufac-
tured women's shoes, bags, and belts in New
York City. By default my father became a
designer, which he remained for most of his
working life. He was a master of form and color.
(This was strange because he was completely
colorblind.) He was also an amazing craftsman.
He was thoughtful and patient and seemed to
have an instinctive understanding of how materiality of every sort behaved.

My parents divorced when I was seven. Soon
thereafter my father began taking me to classi-
cal music concerts, light operas, the ballet,
natural history museums, fancy restaurants,
classic sandwich joints, and places to go horse-
back riding. My mother began taking me to art
museums and galleries, foreign films, delicates-
sens, and pizzerias.

My father never remarried but my mother did. My stepfather was born and raised in Germany. As a young man he was a lawyer. Many of his best friends were associated with the Bauhaus. In 1933, when things got ugly for creative types, my stepfather emigrated to the United States. He changed careers and became a psychoanalyst. My stepfather's hobbies included gardening on hillsides and designing and building houses. He was a terrible craftsman. Curiously, I found his absence of skill combined with his "just-do-it" attitude empowering.

My mother, brother, stepfather, and I lived in a narrow, wooded canyon in the hills above a famously wealthy residential area. We moved there, I always believed, because the natural setting was so beautiful. My mother and stepfather were great admirers of Japanese art and design. Our modest black-painted house was a synthesis of Japanese and rustic Californian design sensibilities.[6]

After returning from a trip to Tokyo in the mid-1960s, my stepfather presented me with a stack of books about Japanese design and architecture. I quickly devoured them. I felt an immediate affinity with the notions of asymmetry, a muted color spectrum, an indifference to American notions of comfort, and the harmonious blending of the manmade with the natural. I was so stimulated that I asked my mother if I could build a Japanese teahouse in a corner of our property. I proceeded to make something quite unorthodox, yet, in terms of atmosphere, it was faithful to the spirit of the earliest Japanese tea-related environments.[7]

Virtually all of the materials I used to construct the teahouse were locally sourced. The cane, bamboo, and eucalyptus wood I personally harvested. The more conventional building elements were scavenged from recently demolished houses. It was the custom of the neighborhood down the hill to raze homes as soon as they were purchased. Even perfectly sound structures were torn down only to have new ones, of the exact same square footage, erected in their place. The only discernible difference between the two homes was the style and/or taste. I thought this was a silly and wasteful practice, but was grateful for the free lumber and hardware.

higher education

I entered university as a philosophy major but soon discovered that the philosophical questions most relevant to me were being raised and addressed in the art department. One of the people I became friendly with there was a teaching assistant in the printmaking division. When I expressed my admiration for one of his prints, he invited me to visit a mural he and another painter were just beginning on the back of an old brick building in Venice (California). A block from the ocean, close to where I lived, I checked it out. It was a trompe l'oeil mirror, a photo-realistic reflection of the street facing the painting. I was so enamored of the concept that I began painting along with them. I then told my best friend, a fellow art student, what we were doing. He also joined in. All together we called ourselves the Los Angeles Fine Arts Squad.

As we stood around admiring our work one afternoon, a flamboyantly dressed man drove up in an outlandish sports car. He introduced himself as the owner of a West Hollywood nightclub located on a busy intersection near Beverly Hills. He asked if we would be interested in painting its exterior. He offered what seemed like a reasonable salary and promised us complete artistic freedom. After discussing the proposition among ourselves, we said yes. Shortly thereafter I dropped out of school.

Determining what to paint on the nightclub's vast, ungainly surface seemed daunting. At the end of a brainstorming session I suggested transposing the story of Siddhartha Gautama, the Indian prince who became the Buddha, to modern-day Los Angeles. My partners liked the idea. It dovetailed perfectly with a belief we all shared: If life has a higher purpose, surely it is to evolve to a more advanced state of consciousness. Through diligent effort and right-mindedness, i.e., meditation and the like, any human being could attain a Buddha-like state of mind in this lifetime.

"Beverly Hills Siddhartha" was the name we gave to this 15,000-square-foot narrative. It took us twelve months to complete. During the three years of its existence, the mural generated tremendous buzz among the art cognoscenti of Los Angeles.[8]

+ + +

When the tedium of painting in our tightly controlled group style became oppressive, I sought other ways of furthering our group's provocative-paintings-in-public-places goal. I approached an art collector friend about financing a 16mm film about our mural-painting process. He agreed on the condition that I collateralize his investment with an artwork from another friend, artist Larry Bell. Should

the documentary fail to recoup the art collector's money, he would get one of Larry's pieces. Larry generously agreed to these terms even though he gained nothing from the deal.

In retrospect it was an absolutely dreadful film, but nobody at the time seemed to notice. With my partners' blessings I took the reel to Europe with the goal of securing another commission. One of the people who viewed the bizarre documentary was connected to the French Ministry of Culture. Amazingly, within a few months, the Squad was invited to Paris. We were given a modest stipend and housed in a magnificent mansion once owned by the writer Honoré de Balzac. (We weren't allowed to use any of the bedrooms. Instead we camped out in sleeping bags on the floor of the grand salon.)

On our first day in the City of Lights we were driven to a park attached to the Château de Vincennes on the outskirts of town. This is where the Paris Biennale, an event billed as "defining the art of the future," was about to be held. We were directed to an enormous wall and told we had six weeks to complete our work. We explained to the Ministry bureau-crats—not once but many times—that the wall was much too large to execute anything nearly as detailed as the "Siddhartha" mural, but nobody wanted to hear this. One of my partners had the idea to paint two painters falling off a scaffold before they had a chance to paint a painting. This was perfect, I thought. We photo-realistically rendered two of my partners dangling from a scaffold against an all-white wall that was faintly gridded with blue chalk lines. (The chalk lines were a central element of a system we used to transfer small photograph-ic images to large walls.) When we ultimately notified the Ministry officials that the mural was complete, they were pleased. When they came to see it, they were furious. The art-viewing public, however, was enchanted.

different aesthetic universes

After working on two-and-a-half murals, it was time to move on. When I told my partners that I was leaving, they weren't surprised.

The absence of a predictable daily routine was liberating at first. The freedom, however, slowly devolved into a kind of dull aimlessness.[9] I yearned for more structured life, so I resolved to go back to school and study architecture. Why architecture? On a symbolic level architecture is, of course, all about creating structure. The impulse, however, probably had more to do with the memory of how my mind had worked when I built my tea house. Wouldn't it be wonderful, I fantasized, to use my brain in that manner to make a living?

Without an undergraduate degree I was fortunate to be admitted into a graduate architecture program.[10] In a perverse expression of gratitude, I spent most of my time in the university's non-architecture-related libraries. I thought that indulging my intellectual curiosity, wherever it led, was the best way to re-find myself. My favorite formal class was a weekly one-on-one tutorial with the head of the botany department. Together we hypothesized the creation of an architecture based on botanical principles. But the more I learned about the real-world practice of architecture, the more apprehensive I became. Architecture seemed much too grounded in "the practical." The scope of creative invention allowed young practitioners seemed far too circumscribed. And the prospect of having to constantly please fickle clients was unsettling. Nevertheless, I stuck it out until I completed all the requirements for the degree. Then, without missing a beat, I reverted to my old art-making ways.[11]

+ + +

In 1975 Venice was a quiet slum by the sea. Nobody paid much attention to what went on there—which made it an ideal place to experiment with just about anything.[12] I resided in a building that had originally been built as a gondola garage. When the once-ubiquitous canals were filled in and paved over, the building was transformed into an automotive garage. When that business folded, a trio of artists purchased the structure and divided it into studio spaces for themselves. What had served as the garage office was converted into an apartment. This is where my girlfriend and I lived.

I supported myself as a photographer. I created slightly surreal images for record album covers. I also photographed building interiors and exteriors for architects and shelter magazines. I lived modestly and had a lot of free time. Most of my friends and acquaintances were either artists or in some way connected with the arts.

I had a strong desire to make art too but strug-gled with the content and form my art should take. I only knew it had to be completely differ-ent from anything that I had ever seen or expe-rienced before.

Typically, I spent one or two afternoons a week visiting the studios of other artists in the hope of gleaning whatever inspiration I could. Every Venice studio hid behind an anonymous facade. And inside every studio there was an artist exploring what seemed like novel aesthetic terrain:

Billy Al Bengston produced watercolors. Each featured either a stylized lily or a chevron, his two signature images at the time. I thought Billy Al's paintings were pretty. I meant that in a good way.[13] I once caught Billy Al painting while watching soap operas on TV. That seemed weird, but who was I to judge? When Billy Al intoned, "There is never enough beauty in the world," I was sure he was on to something important.

Laddie John Dill made cement paintings: large, heavy paintings composed of poured cement. He worked on a dozen or so at a time on the floor of his voluminous space. While the cement was still wet, he moved from painting to painting, here and there adding shards of broken glass and patches of color pigment. His systematic, factory-like manner of production made me think of his art as a kind of aesthetically pleasing industrial product. I found this a provocative notion.

Bryan Hunt carved precise, dirigible-shaped forms out of balsa wood. It was the kind of thing a geeky model-building kid might do. He then covered them with silk paper and thin metal leaf. He mounted the completed pieces nose first, high on his studio walls. They looked like elegant airships docked in space. I was

impressed with Bryan's ability to get gallerists and collectors to buy into his highly specific vision.

Alexis Smith composed strings of words that came together as nonsensical prose. They were drawn or painted on long lengths of paper pinned to her studio wall. I found her artwork poetic but extremely opaque. I was inspired by her resolute commitment to an abstruse sensibility.

Eric Orr seemed more interested in creating temporary pieces than permanent objects. One of his short-lived installations was a small enclosed maze that led to a room-like center space. I found it captivating. He first construct-ed it in his studio, then on the beach. It was thrilling to be in a "room" with walls of card-board, a floor of sand, and a ceiling of blue sky.

Of all the art made in Venice, I responded to Tom Wudl's the most. Tom painted on what appeared to be large sheets of tissue paper. With a hammer and die he then punched holes—one hole at a time—uniformly over the surface. Thus perforated, the paintings became even more ethereal. Beyond whatever idea content it had, I was convinced that Tom's art had an intrinsic extra-added value due to the painstaking hand labor expended in its making.

Peter Alexander was the artist I had the greatest intellectual affinity with. Like me he was an architecture-school graduate who found art a better outlet for his creative energies. Early in his career he achieved commercial success with a series of Minimalist cast-resin sculptures that bent light in a puzzling way. The artworks were obviously solid, but they appeared to be fluid or jelly-like too. Peter could have gone on making and selling slightly different iterations of these pieces forever, but he lost interest.

Instead he began making pastel drawings of wondrous, exaggerated sunsets—which also became highly coveted by collectors. Then, once again, he changed media and subject matter. This time he affixed swatches of flexible colored resin, pieces of costume jewelry, exotic fabrics, glitter, and other small shiny objects onto lengths of draped black velvet. At the time black velvet was associated mainly with the kitsch paintings of bullfighters sold in Mexican tourist shops. It wasn't really a "proper" medium for "serious" artists.

I found Peter's "velvets" intriguing. The soft, dense, silky materiality was sensuous, suggestive, alluring. But did Peter's collage-like additions really transform the material into convincing artworks? Was there something truly new and conceptually interesting here? Or were the "velvets" merely "decorative"? Each time I visited his studio, Peter seemed to be pondering a different facet of the same questions.

Grappling with complex subjective concerns like these was, I thought, the crux of an artist's job. I viewed it as the artist acting as a midwife at the birth of a new understanding of beauty.[14]

wetness

When it was my turn to advance a new understanding of beauty, I homed in on the concept of absurdity. For me, the ultimate absurdity was the fundamental human condition: Nature's only discernible goal for us is to stay alive long enough to reproduce, raise our young, and then, when our young are old enough to repeat the process, get out of the way. There is nothing more for us to do. Yet because our lifespans are so extended—all the while we remain conscious and full of energy—we invent stories, amusements, obligations, and myriad other ruses to occupy ourselves and to provide a distraction from the reality of this reality.

I thought that bathing—the act of bathing in all its silly-to-sacred manifestations—could serve as a proxy not only for the essential absurdity that underlies our lives but also for the ingenious ways in which we distract ourselves from awareness of it. I began producing what I called "bath art" to explore these ideas. I photographed friends and acquaintances bathing in unusual situations. I used these images as the elements of more complex compositions. I reproduced them as lithographic and silkscreen prints.[15] I sold them through word of mouth and through a tiny poster and print gallery run by a novice gallerist named Larry Gagosian.

Around this time, while riding my bicycle though a nondescript area of Venice, I chanced upon a curious poster stapled to a utility pole. Initially I thought it was an announcement for an upcoming boxing match. Graphics of this sort were common in the working-class districts of L.A. In this instance, however, instead of a prizefighter's mug and torso, there was an attractive young woman in a strapless top crouching down to pick up a handful of writing implements. The headline blared "200 Black Pens." In less emphatic script just below it read,

"Inscribed on each pen is this sentence: 'The attitude of the two had a terrible resemblance to a child forcing a kitten's nose into a saucer of milk to compel it to drink.'" And in small type at the bottom it said, "MORALITY IMMORALITY AND MYTHOLOGICAL SCIENCE. Denise is no angel, but she will have her wings." Nothing about the poster made any sense. Its incongruous appearance in an obscure neighborhood and the absence of any authorial responsibility compounded the absurdity.[16] I found this all very exciting, but I also felt challenged. Now I had to push the bathing-absurdity trope to a higher level. The result was *WET: The Magazine of Gourmet Bathing*.

+ + +

The simplest explanation of *WET* is that it was a work of art about absurdity disguised as a "real" (as opposed to an "art") magazine. The people who "got" *WET* without having it explained

Why Even Try

were mainly artists and similar creative types. This was *WET*'s natural audience. "Regular" people were often baffled. "A magazine about 'gourmet bathing'? Really? Why?" In the early days of *WET*, I often reminded myself that art doesn't have to be easily understood. Nor does it even have to "make sense."

And "gourmet bathing"? This was the conjoining of two unrelated words that providentially popped into my head while taking a bath. In practical usage "gourmet bathing" was an elusive, infinitely malleable meme that I employed to amplify *WET*'s underlying ambiguity. This is to say, "gourmet bathing" was a chameleon-like concept that meant virtually anything.

On a macro level *WET*, like that challenging artwork masquerading as a common street poster, was designed to exist outside of conventional art contexts. *WET* was sold in supermarkets, record and surf shops, clothing stores, and gift boutiques—but not in art galleries, museums, or establishments that sold "artist books." *WET*'s effectiveness as an artwork was due, in part, to its refusal to be tied down or boxed into any standard frames of reference.[17]

welcome to japan!

Toward the end of *WET*'s five-and-a-half-year run, journalists from Japanese lifestyle publications became a regular fixture in the *WET* offices. Why were the Japanese so interested in what we were doing, I wondered.[18] I owed myself a vacation, so I booked a flight to Tokyo to find out. From the moment I stepped onto the tarmac at Haneda Airport, I became so mesmerized by the materiality of this new culture that I completely forgot my stated mission.

Everywhere my gaze fell seemed familiar, yet also unfamiliar. It was like being in a science fiction movie where one small change in a minor detail of the past alters everything in the present. The toilet in my hotel room, for instance.[19] It looked exactly like the one in my Venice apartment except that it had a goose-neck-shaped faucet rising atop the water tank.

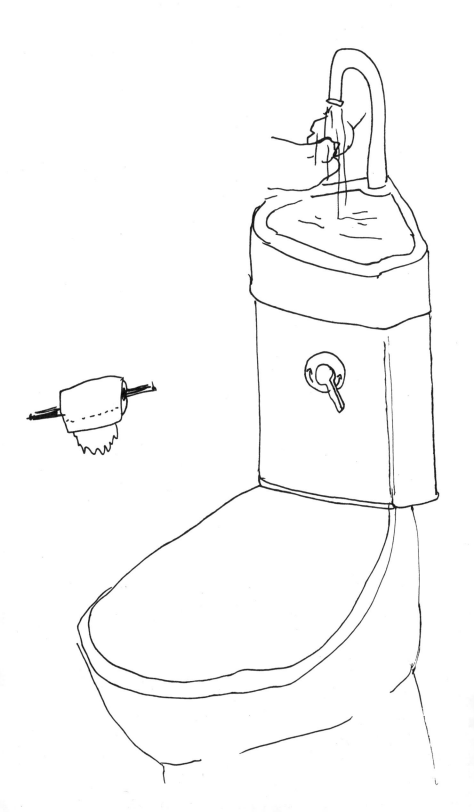

When the toilet flushed, water flowed out of this faucet and down into a hole in the tank lid refilling the tank for the next flush. The falling water was for washing my hands, but it took my befuddled mind a while to figure this out. When I finally understood I wasn't washing my hands in toilet water, I began to appreciate the cleverness of this graywater recycling scheme. I saw this same kind of down-to-earth, conservation-minded intelligence repeated over and over again in every manner of Japanese functional object.

+ + +

When I wasn't exploring the surface of Tokyo, I was meeting with Japanese creators. Artist-illustrator Yumura Teruhiko (aka Flamingo Terry, King Terry, et al.) was one of the most memorable. Yumura was a pioneer of the *heta-uma* style of drawing, painting, and sculpture. *Heta uma*—literally "bad tasty" or "clumsy good"—

looks like the inept gesturings of a child. On closer inspection though, a sophisticated mind with a wicked sense of humor is obviously at play. *Heta-uma* is, in effect, bad taste recast as high cool.

Because of our shared artistic enthusiasms, Yumura invited me to visit his studios. The larger one was located in an old wooden house slated for imminent demolition. Yumura insisted that I walk on the tatami-matted floors in my street shoes. Everyone did, he said. Since shoes are forbidden in Japanese homes, this was an audacious breach of a societal taboo, so I was apprehensive. But then the experience was bouncy, like walking on the moon, and I became giddy.

Yumura's other studio was next door in a small, white, cube-like concrete building. Here the full range of his *heta-uma* production was carted out: clothing, books, bags, mooks, stationery, video, food packaging, etc. I was in awe. Yumura good-humoredly mentioned that "interesting opportunities" happen for proven creators in Japan. I found this possibility so enticing that when I shut *WET* down half a year later, I headed back to Tokyo as soon as I could.[20]

+ + +

After learning that *WET* was no more, an editor at a popular Japanese men's lifestyle magazine inquired if I would write articles for his publication. He asked me to first outline my ideas. I politely declined. After the freedom I enjoyed at *WET*, having my ideas vetted before exploring them felt regressive. Instead I offered to produce a bimonthly column about whatever I found interesting wherever I happened to be. I suggested "Dr. Leonardo's Guide to Cultural Anthropology" as the title. The editor liked the concept and all of sudden I had a steady income.[21]

Around this same time I was introduced to Kioshi Shikita, an affable man about my age who was connected to the worlds of Japanese fashion and avant-garde music.[22] He dressed like a sly, ironic Tokyo hipster. I was entranced by the hyper-fastidious way he entered information into his pocket-sized appointment book. (He wrote with a mechanical pencil in the smallest-yet-legible script I had ever seen.) We instantly hit it off and he became my agent. Within a month I was commissioned to make music videos for a Tokyo-based television station. Later I was hired to come up with the music and images for a feature-length video sold through a trendy Japanese department store chain.

fashion

As I moved about Tokyo by subway, by train, and on foot, something unusual registered on my radar. Lots of people in their 20s, 30s, and 40s wore asymmetrically cut clothing that didn't conform to or flatter their body shapes. These garments, which covered almost everything, were mainly in shades of gray and black. I found this sexy. Rather, I found the people who wore those clothes sexy. This, I thought, was interesting. Back in Los Angeles, exposed skin and a shapely body—overt sexual messaging—was the predominant erotic flavor. In Tokyo though, this unfamiliar eroticism was rooted in a person's confident and self-assured manner. Somehow these clothes supported these attitudes. How, I wondered? Serendipitously, my agent phoned and asked if I'd like to accompany him to an important fashion show. He said the company's name was Comme des Garçons.[23]

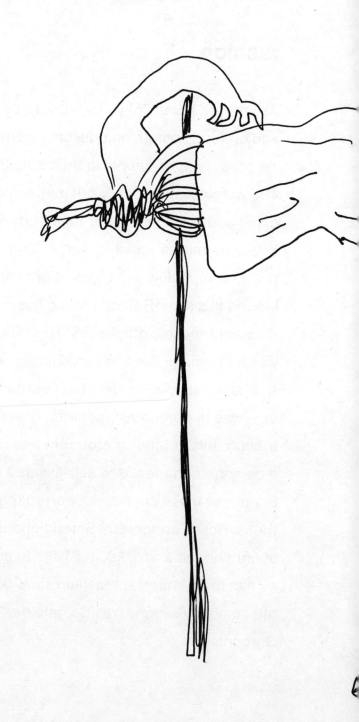

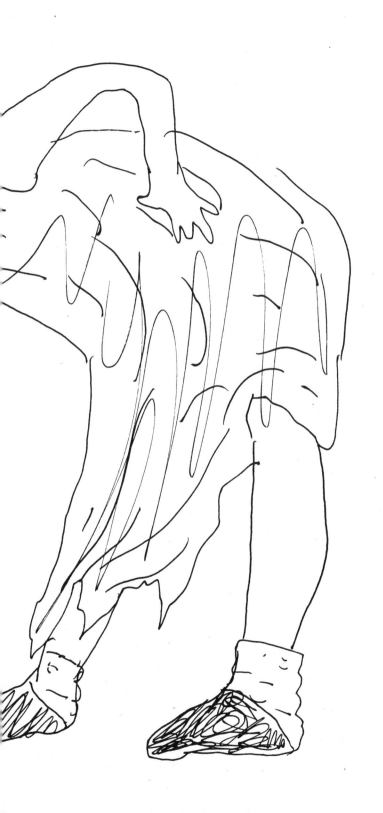

The venue was an elegant gray tent temporarily erected beside one of Japan's most recognizable buildings, a stunning structure left over from the 1964 Tokyo Olympics.[24] All of the attendees were attired in shades of either gray or black. There was much chatter, but all in hushed, respectful tones. The atmosphere was solemn, like that of a religious convocation—until the performance began. Fifteen heartbeats into the thump-thump music, tall, mostly Western models began strutting down the elevated runway. All of their hair was outlandishly styled. All of their faces had been streaked with harsh, strident strokes of color. It was sensual, but in an austere, almost ascetic way. Then there were the clothes: Every garment boldly proclaimed a new aesthetic order. Up until that moment I had cared little for fashion per se, yet it was exhilarating to be among so many who responded to every garment detail as if it were a revelation.

It took a few weeks for everything to sink in. From what I could piece together, a thousand years of Japanese-clothing tradition was, at that very instant, converging with the Western fashion idiom for the very first time. Simply put, an aesthetic revolution was underway and I was at ground zero. As I awoke from a nap one afternoon, I was seized by an intense desire to spread the news. Intuitively I thought a book would be the perfect vehicle. It would be my first book.[25] How to proceed? I cobbled together some fanciful words and colorful drawings and took them to an editor at the English-language division of Japan's largest publishing company. He liked my proposal and convinced his superiors to offer me a contract. Throughout the ensuing project the editor, who later became a friend, was incredibly supportive. He arranged for an assistant to help me gain entry into some spectacular historical photo archives. (He also shielded me from his company's interminable intra-office squabbling and turf issues.)

Fashion, I quickly learned, doesn't demand a studied investigation into deeper meanings as, say, art does. To the perceptive eye everything relevant is pretty much on the surface. Thus, it was relatively easy to connect the dots and put together a taxonomy of Japan's approach to fashion/clothing design from the ancient past to the current moment. When the press and public relations staff at the leading fashion houses learned what I was up to, I was treated like a new best friend. I was granted as much access as I needed to all the key designers and, of course, I was invited to all the fashion shows. With so much good will and encouragement, the various elements of my project came together in an almost frictionless way.[26] By the time my volume was at the printer, I had completely fallen in love with the book-making process.[27]

making books

Publishing a book was logistically much more straightforward than producing a magazine. I could make a book anywhere, all by myself. Or, I could solicit as much or as little help from others as I wanted. Making a book required little physical space. (I had put the fashion book together almost entirely on my bed.)[28] And books didn't really have absolute deadlines. I could set my own schedule and change it if need be. Furthermore, book publishing didn't entail chasing potential advertisers. My first six books were published by large established companies. I was paid an advance against future royalties, so I didn't have to continually fret about where the money was coming from.

I had entered the book industry at a propitious moment. But that was about to change. Risk-averse sales and marketing people were beginning to replace idea-loving editors as the industry's prime decision makers. I found this uncomfortable, then impossible. My books were unconventional. They needed a supportive, open-minded publishing infrastructure. I had to find another, more sympathetic manner of producing and distributing books or find a new expressive medium. Out of desperation I considered independent publishing. I knew the rudiments of the business. If I strictly adhered to the "cheap is good" philosophy we hewed to at *WET*, I reckoned, things might work out okay.

+ + +

During an excursion to a hot springs resort near the seaside city of Kamakura, about an hour south of Tokyo, the subject of my first independently published book effortlessly materialized. After disrobing but before rinsing off and entering the large outdoor pool, I took a leisurely look around at what my fellow bathers were up to. Everyone was following the same basic procedure, yet there were significant variations. Had I been unfamiliar with the Japanese bathing ritual, I might have been confused. If *I* were confused, surely other non-Japanese would be confused too. In fact, the longer I observed my fellow bathers, the more un-simple this ostensibly simple routine seemed. It struck me that a book with explicit instructions, conveyed primarily through illustrations, might make a useful little volume. While immersed in the hot mineral water, I mentally configured the book's structure. By the time I was dressed and ready to leave, I had completely sketched out the book's pictorial scheme.

By a stroke of luck, the editor of my Japanese fashion book had moved to California and had started his own small publishing company. I asked if I could publish *How to Take a Japanese Bath* through his imprint, and he agreed. [29] The book ended up selling reasonably well.

Emboldened, I set to work on a follow-up volume using the same format. The illustrator, a manga artist revered for his evocative retro-style drawings, was the same too.[30] The book's title was its subject: *How To Rake Leaves*. Again, the idea had come unbidden: I was staring out over the endless expanse of Tokyo from the third-floor window of an office building situated on a slight rise. It was a chilly autumn evening with a hint of bittersweet melancholy in the air. Playfully I mused about the brittle, desiccated leaves that were gently falling to the ground. With pencil in hand I imagined what it would be like living in a small Cape Cod-style cottage surrounded by a leaf-covered lawn in the middle of this hideously beautiful metropolis. Miraculously, this book sold well too.

+ + +

After the relative success of my first two independently published books, I felt a need to go deeper. I wanted the subject of my next book to address a vague, hard-to-put-my-finger-on aesthetic concept of passionate personal concern. I wanted my approach to be honest, original, intellectually rigorous, yet crystal clear. How could I meld all these requirements? After muddling through a mishmash of methodological approaches, I ended up focusing on the beauty of a single autumn leaf randomly picked up on the street. The process of entropy was well underway. The leaf was beautiful but it was approaching nothingness. . . . Beauty . . . Nothingness . . . On the way to nothingness . . . At the edge of nothingness . . . Beauty at the edge of nothingness . . . I played with these ideas until I arrived at a particularly resonant sound bite: the beauty of things imperfect, impermanent, and incomplete. I called the concept wabi-sabi, the conjoining of two ancient Japanese words, *wabi* and *sabi*. Through the pro-

cess of discovering, elaborating on, and sys-
tematizing what wabi-sabi was, I had created
my first conceptual tool.[31]

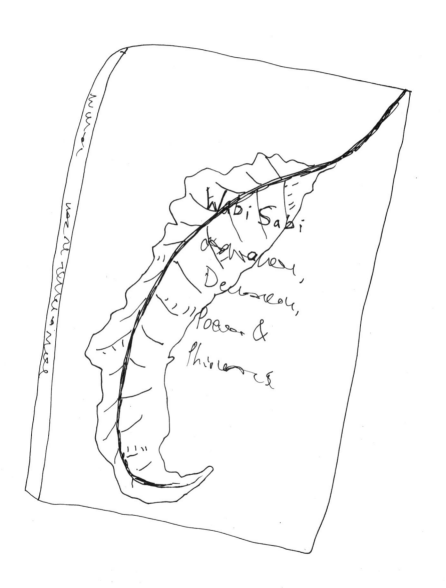

Wabi Sabi
of Chocolate,
Decadence,
Power &
Philosophy

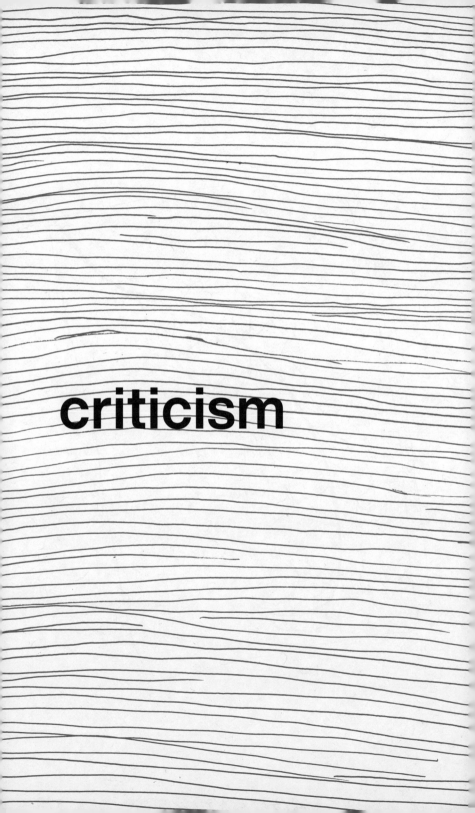

criticism

the dream is over

During my early days in Tokyo, I often heard locals say, "We are a poor country. . . ." Japan seemed to have everything a reasonable person could possibly want, but I understood what they meant. Compared with the visible affluence of many Western countries, the Japanese felt a need to apologize because their country wasn't "there" yet. Ironically, I liked Japan precisely because it wasn't "there" yet. Indeed, the kind of Japanese beauty I fell most in love with was the result of meticulous attention paid to transforming modest, humble materials into the refined, affordable-for-all objects of everyday life.

During this period I rented a room in an inexpensive-but-well-maintained wooden apartment building of a type called an apato. Apatos were then common, particularly in the older areas of town. They provided a way for the economically disadvantaged to live frugally in the big city. My

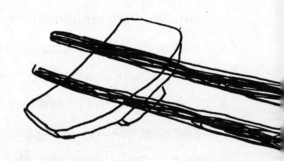

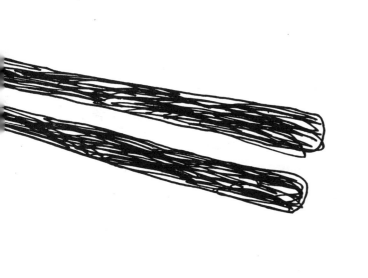

room consisted of eight tatami mats, approximately 150 square feet. Included in that space was a pared-down kitchen. All of the rooms in my building were the exact same size and layout. At the end of the central hall on each floor was a toilet shared by all. There were no bathing facilities, but the local public bath was a mere two blocks away.

I used my room only during the day and only for work.[32] However, for the building's other occupants it was where they ate, slept, and socialized. All the interior and exterior walls were thin and uninsulated. When it was cold outside, it was cold inside. When it was hot outside, it was hot inside. Between the rooms there was compete visual separation, but if you sneezed in one unit, it could be heard in all the others. In spite of this lack of thermal comfort and acoustical privacy, I could have happily lived there full time if some of my friends or professional peers had too.

+ + +

Midway through my stay in Japan, I began
noticing a marked shift in cultural attitudes.[33]
Tokyo's apatos began disappearing, as did most
of the other old residential and commercial
buildings made of wood. New structures of
concrete and synthetic composites were erected in their place. A culture-wide reappraisal of
traditional aesthetic values seemed to be
underway. On a social level changes were also
afoot. A boorish arrogance began supplanting
the gentle Japanese humility I was so fond of.
Japan was becoming a "normal" country.

One of the people I encountered during this
transitional period was an ambitious fine-arts
photographer who had a side business as an
antiques dealer. He also considered himself an
interior designer. I once met with him in the
Tokyo apartment he had designed for himself. I
also visited a private office he had designed for

his girlfriend, the owner of an uptown art gallery. I thought he was an exceptionally clever photographer but a merely competent designer. I was quite surprised when, many years later, I came across an extensive article in a prestigious design/lifestyle magazine about an apartment he had created for a wealthy married couple in Manhattan.[34]

The photographs accompanying the text showed a quasi-traditional Japanese interior with pronounced Minimalist and Mid-Century Modern tweaks. It followed a predictable design scheme that I had seen innumerable times before. The difference in this instance was that the apartment was atop one of the tallest luxury skyscrapers in the world. It occupied an entire floor, almost 8,000 square feet. The apartment was so high that it had unobstructed views of Central Park to the north, Midtown and Lower Manhattan to the south, Brooklyn and Queens to the east, and the Hudson River and

New Jersey to the west. If so desired, the specially fabricated window coverings could be adjusted to completely blot out the city—leaving only the sky and the clouds.

The transformation from raw space to completed interior took four years. According to the magazine, the photographer/designer insisted on using as many "premodern" Japanese materials and techniques as possible: Precious and difficult-to-obtain sorts of wood. (Planks from one-thousand-year-old trees grown in a remote forest on a tiny island, for example.) Stones from centuries-old Japanese gardens. Stones recycled from a Kyoto tram station. A precious variety of handmade Japanese ceramic tiles. An uncommon type of metal wall surface. And on and on. All of these rarefied materials were shipped from Japan. Specialized Japanese craftsmen were then flown to New York to perform the extensive detail work. . . .

The apartment was unquestionably newswor-
thy. It was extraordinary in many ways: The
unique center-of-the-world location. The painstaking attention to details. The enormous
implicit expense. Yet, it was ordinary in many
ways too. It was a common example of extreme
wealth flaunting its ability to satisfy its every
capricious whim, oblivious of—or indifferent
to—the consequences. (The project's huge
carbon footprint, for instance. The incitement
of envy . . .) The article seemed to advance a
narrative about good taste, specialness, and
even enlightened aestheticism. What I perceived instead was a betrayal of the unpreten-
tious spirit lying at the heart of truly great
Japanese design. Modesty, humility, and
unfussy refinement had been unceremoniously
shoved aside. Ostentation took their place.

accepting responsibility

I have strong opinions about things aesthetic.
Doesn't everyone? Making judgments about
style and taste—what's good, what's bad—is
one of the ways we fill up our lives with meaning. Nevertheless, I try to temper the manner in
which I express my opinions (the previous
paragraph notwithstanding). Harsh words can
be hurtful, and being intentionally hurtful is
ugly. However, when something is purposely
cast into the public arena, isn't criticism, both
positive or negative, being implicitly invited?

With the foregoing in mind, I want to discuss an
irksome problem I confronted involving an
expensive chair. I had purchased the chair
shortly after leaving my Japanese life behind. I
bought it because it embodied a beautiful
structural principle, a beautiful idea that I wanted to re-experience every day. It wasn't very
comfortable, as iconic chairs often aren't, so I

rarely sat in it. That is why I was so surprised when the chair's glue joints—the chair was put together entirely with glue—began failing one right after another over a span of a few months. It wasn't just my chair that was deconstructing though. I noticed the same chair gracefully falling apart in the homes of friends too. Even the chair displayed in the permanent collection of our local museum of modern art was disassembling. Before I bought the chair, I had expressly questioned the efficacy of the construction method. The salesperson confidently reassured me that it was "airplane glue" and that the bonds would outlast us both.

When I called the manufacturer to see what could be done, I was told, "Sorry, your five-year warranty has lapsed." Interestingly though, I was offered preprinted repair instructions. This made me curious. If there were repair instructions, that meant the manufacturer knew of the problem. If they were aware of the problem, why didn't they fix it? Or, if that wasn't possible, remove the chair from the market?

It wasn't so simple, I discovered. This beautiful chair, designed by an internationally famous architect, was an important component of the company's marketing/brand-identity strategy. It was introduced to the product line with much fanfare at a time when the manufacturer needed something provocative to reassert its relevance in the design world. The real problem, as I saw it, was that it wasn't really well designed. Saying that a chair is well designed means, among other things, that it will function as advertised over a long period of time. By "function" I don't just mean symbolically or aesthetically, but also in an actual utilitarian manner.[35] Shouldn't durability be an especially important feature of pricey chairs? This chair's de facto planned obsolescence—which the failing glue joints insured—was clearly a big negative.

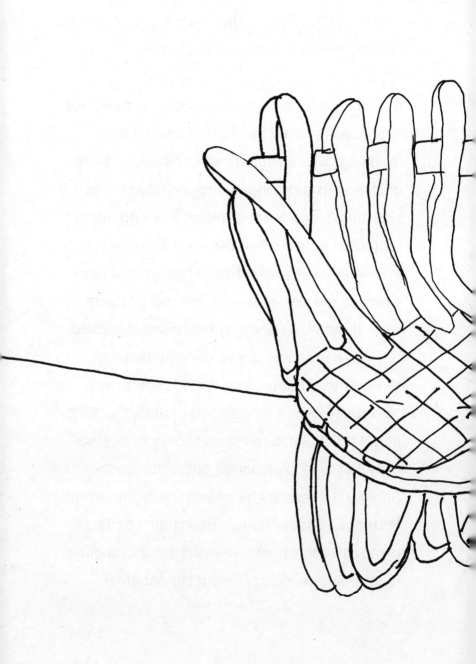

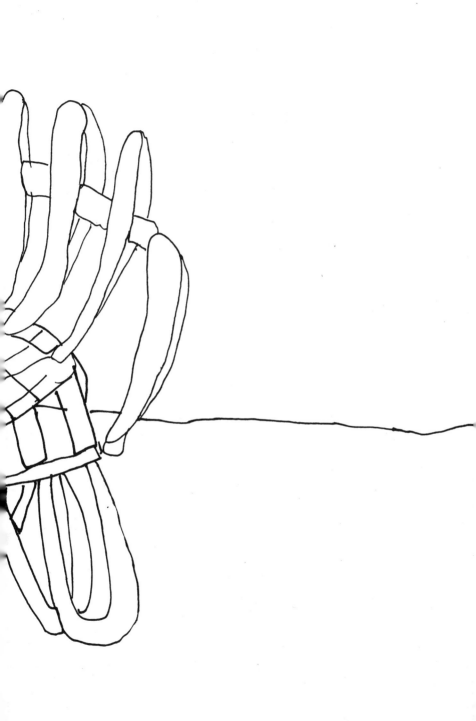

Following many polite letters and courteous phone calls, I was finally able to speak with a company vice president. After vainly trying to get him to admit that there was a serious design miscalculation and that the marketing for the chair was disingenuous, I asked why his company didn't just call the chair a work of art? If it was an artwork, longevity (and even comfort) would no longer be an issue. He tacitly acknowledged my point, but his strategic silences indicated that this was not an option.

I was such a persistent nuisance that the company eventually did repair my chair at their expense.[36] However, within a few months it began completely deconstructing once again. What could I do but laugh? It was only a chair, after all. So why did I spend so much time and energy seeking redress for what I perceived to be an "aesthetic wrong"? It was not the flawed chair design that irked me. It was the company's deliberate dereliction of its responsibility to its customers that I perceived as the real aesthetic wrong. If I, an aesthete, don't make an effort to uphold aesthetic standards and values I believe in, who will? I am quite certain that in the end it doesn't really matter at all. But it is not the end. It is now. And now is always a good time to act responsibly.

questionable beauty

Having been seduced into buying a ridiculous chair because of the beauty of its structural principle, what should I have learned, if anything, about using beauty as a guide to making wise choices?

+ + +

When talking with customer service representatives of large corporations, I often hear expressions of kindness, courtesy, respect, and sometimes even empathy and concern. "I am very sorry to hear that." "I certainly understand how you feel." "We take your blah-blah-blah very seriously." These are beautiful words to assuage my frustration, my feelings of neglect, and perhaps even my anger. Should I trust the sincerity and honesty of these beautiful words?

+ + +

IS BEA

Merely A

COATiNG

REAL

UTY

SÜGAR-

ON HARSH

TIES ?

An ardent environmental activist, who also believed in the importance of beauty, once financed a book about the horrors of clearcut logging. The book was filled with images of denuded forests, all beautifully photographed. The photographs were so gorgeous that I found myself questioning, "Is clearcut logging really that bad?"

+ + +

The idea of glorifying torture is repugnant to me. But beautiful artistry can sometimes quell or overpower my moral qualms. If I am at the Prado, the Uffizi, or the Met and happen upon an exquisite rendering of Jesus on a cross—nails through his hands and feet, a crown of thorns tearing into his flesh, an anguished look on his face—am I, in a secular context, a hypocrite if I linger in front of that painting and experience aesthetic pleasure?

+ + +

As a thought experiment, let's assume that the ability to perceive beauty evolved through natural selection to help our ancestors make prudent, survival-related decisions. Beauty was then a marker of the healthy and the good. But not always. Snakes, tigers, and shiny red mushrooms with little white dots on top were beautiful, but also dangerous. This could be confusing to a fatal degree. Fortunately we are now so sophisticated that we are able to recognize danger even when it is packaged beautifully. Or can we? As the sun rises and falls through thick layers of polluted air, most of us reflexively "ooh" and "ahh" at the surreal beauty of the super-intense maroons and ever-deeper purples. What happens next?

making nothing

The Ancient Greeks believed that the worst
fate that could possibly befall a human being
was to live a life utterly devoid of meaning.
This, anyway, is what I deduced from my reading of the myth of Sisyphus. In this well-known
allegory, Sisyphus, an exceedingly clever and
arrogant man, tricks and humiliates the gods
one too many times. As punishment, Zeus
condemns Sisyphus to an eternity of futile
labor: Sisyphus must push a heavy rock up a
steep hill. And every time the rock gets almost
to the top of the hill, it rolls back down. Sisyphus must then push it back up again, and
again, and again, and again—forever.

(But what if Sisyphus, resourceful to the core,
had figured out a way to imbue his futile labors
with meaning?)

+ + +

On a brilliant autumn afternoon when the sky was blue and the temperature mild, I was inspired to do some outdoor housekeeping. Leaves, twigs, and other vegetable matter had piled up on the wood and concrete steps that ran through our garden. I realized, of course, that as soon as I finished removing this debris it would immediately return. I was okay with that. I have accepted a quasi-Sisyphean view of things. After selecting an appropriate broom and collection basket, I began my work. My pace was slow and measured. The stairs were irregular and cracked in places, so I moved even more slowly so as not to miss any of the bits and pieces crammed into the nooks and crannies. Why rush anyway? I was beginning to enjoy this.

Sweeping up nature's refuse isn't typically considered an act of exceptional consequence. I knew this. So I was surprised when a peculiar idea insinuated itself front and center into my awareness: "With every sweep of this broom I am restoring order. And by restoring order—if only momentarily—I am saving the universe."

It was a crazy notion, of that I was certain. Nevertheless, it felt as true as anything I had ever believed. How, I wondered, could this be? Later that day an answer came: Just as nature has given us a mind capable of perceiving our role in the overarching scheme of existence, nature has also given us a mind capable of creating meaning out of just about anything. Furthermore, nature has given us a mind with the ability to *believe* that the meanings we create are actually true.

+ + +

The following summer, in order to detach ourselves from the modern world, my wife, son, and I went to stay in the unglamorous Italian hilltop town where my in-laws live. I mainly ate with family and friends, slept, read, and took multiple daily walks. During these walks my mind became active, but not too active. I noticed things though. Specifically, I noticed that there was lots of litter on the ground: along the roads, in empty lots, and even in the fields and forests that surrounded the town. Litter, trash, garbage, debris, refuse, waste, detritus—each denotes an undesirable state of materiality. Something no longer wanted. Something to get rid of.

Almost instinctually I began picking up the discarded soft drink containers, cigarette boxes, empty water bottles, and other tossed-off product packaging that I encountered during my walks. And, when I came across a (rare) trash receptacle, I deposited my collection.

As is my custom, I began hatching theories regarding the motives for my behavior. Maybe I hoped that when the townspeople and tourists saw what I was doing, they would reconsider their actions and clean up after themselves. Or, recalling my autumnal epiphany, perhaps I was simply trying to restore a little order and, by so doing, saving, if not the universe, at least a tiny corner of our planet.

+ + +

The notion of "saving" things is rooted in my long-time obsession with trying to find ways of making "nothing" in a manner that is remunerative. After reading a magazine article about the work of a nineteenth-century English economist named William Stanley Jevons, this preoccupation took on an even greater urgency.[37] Jevons observed the following: When an innovative new technology (James Watt's steam engine in Jevons's case) causes a resource (coal) to be used more efficiently, the price per unit of energy derived from this resource decreases. Thereafter the demand for this resource increases as entrepreneurs and others find new uses for it. This phenomenon is now known as the Jevons paradox or Jevons effect. It is controversial, but many economists still think it is operational today. This made me wonder: What will happen when technological advancements in wind- and solar-power generation trigger a dramatic drop in the price of electricity? Will much cheaper electricity precipitate a boom in the manufacture and consumption of devices and machines that use this energy? Don't we produce way too much stuff already? This is when I began to appreciate that making nothing is one of the most meaningful things a person can do.

+ + +

How do you make "nothing" and support yourself doing so? Imagination is the key. The way artist John Cage (1912–92) did it is a good example. Cage's primary medium was sound, but his most enduring artwork is about silence, a form of nothing. The title of the piece is "4'33"." At its premier performance in 1952, a formally dressed pianist walked over to a piano, sat down, and pulled out a stopwatch. He then opened the keyboard cover, sat motionless, then closed it. He followed this routine three times marking three intervals of silence that altogether lasted 4 minutes and 33 seconds. Cage, in his recollection of that evening, noted that "You could hear the wind stirring outside during the first movement. During the second, raindrops began pattering the roof. And during the third the people themselves made all kinds of interesting sounds as they talked or walked out." The audience found that even in ostensible silence—nothing—there were tremendous opportunities for something to exist.

Cage later remarked that he had worked longer and harder on creating and crafting "4'33"" than on any of his other compositions. The

piece has subsequently been performed countless times by countless other people. It has
become legendary in the art world and beyond.
It greatly boosted Cage's artistic reputation.
And that, in the material world, is fungible.

+ + +

In the so-called real world, outside of the
domains of art and other forms of fanciful
thinking, how does making nothing and sup-
porting oneself doing so really work? I could
never figure that out. So after my return from
Italy, where money isn't everything, I altered the
parameters of my query. It became, "How does
one make something *meaningful* by making
nothing?" Then some insights came.

Going about my daily rounds I ran into Jonathan, a neighbor and local hero. Jonathan
wears many hats. One of them is that of a
land-use activist. Over the decades Jonathan

has been amazingly effective in helping convert unused private lands to public use. Jonathan was also instrumental in blocking the construction of a residential development in a nearby forest, thereby leaving the land intact. Had that project proceeded we would have suffered a blighted landscape at best, an environmental disaster at worst. I thanked Jonathan profusely for this beautiful thing he had accomplished, but he responded wistfully. "Unfortunately, people rarely appreciate things they cannot see."

"This is true," I concurred. Beauty is typically associated with bringing new things into existence: A beautiful painting. A beautiful musical composition. Beautiful architecture . . . But beauty, I realized at that instant, can also be created and/or restored by removing things from existence. Like eliminating the visible consequences of thoughtless human action. That is what I did when picking up litter in and around that unglamorous Italian hilltop town. Jonathan, however, did something even more significant, more beautiful, and more meaningful. He had prevented thoughtless human action from occurring in the first place. He made nothing by insuring that nothing would be made.

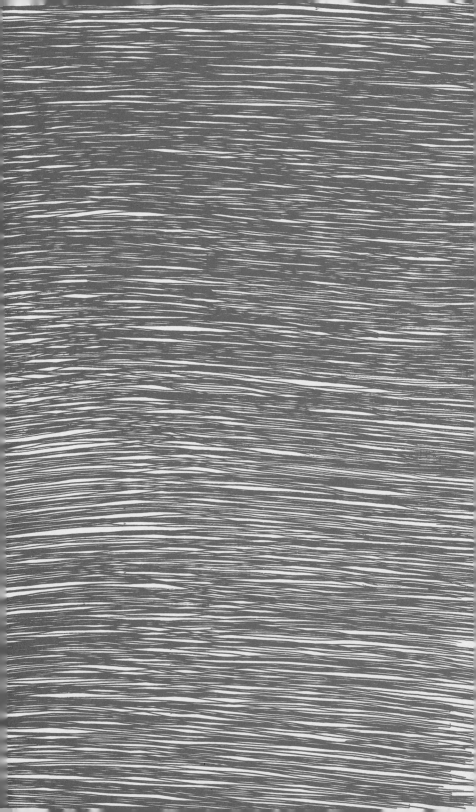

the beautiful human being

Mother, you were born
so I was born.
You will die
and I will follow you there.
How can I thank you,
all this time
preparing the ground?

—Peter Levitt, from *One Hundred Butterflies* [38]

+ + +

I was comfortably seated at a picnic table in the
Northern California backyard of my friends
Greg and Marta. I had been invited there for
lunch. Marta had just returned from New York
and was anxious to tell me about her trip. This
is what I remember her relating:

While in New York Marta had stayed at the tenth-floor Midtown Manhattan apartment of a friend. On the last day of her visit, as she glanced out the window, she saw a man standing on a ledge of the building directly across the street. He was in his underwear. As she looked closer, Marta realized that the man was screaming for help. . . . A chorus of sirens soon filled the air. As the firemen unloaded their gear, an amplified voice from the street below bellowed, "Help is on the way! Stay put! Don't move!" Time passed and smoke began issuing from the windows behind the man. The promised help, however, had not arrived. The man was frantic. Then hysterical. Then he jumped.

By the end of her grim recital, Marta was visibly shaken. I was numb. After a quiet meal together, I drove back home as if in a trance.

Later that evening I received an unexpected phone call. It was from a former friend whom I hadn't heard from—or thought about—in ages. In the interim she had married, had a child, and divorced. She sounded stressed. I asked what was wrong. She said that her ex-husband had stopped paying the alimony he owed. Plus, she had lost her job and was having trouble finding a new one. Also, she had recently moved into a new apartment, but without the alimony the rent was unaffordable. The prospect of eviction was terrifying. On top of all that, she and her now-adult daughter were estranged. "I'm completely exhausted," she lamented. "I don't know how much longer I can go on like this." I took this to mean that she was contemplating something extreme, perhaps even final.

Toward the end of her woeful account, I began wrestling with the ethical calculus. Why is she calling me after all these years? There is nothing connecting us anymore. I certainly don't have any obligation or responsibility for her well-being. Or do I? Then I remembered Marta's macabre tale. Sometimes terrible things happen right before your eyes and there is nothing you can do. That was Marta's situation. What about the inverse? What if you know that something horrible might occur and there is something you can do? This was my dilemma. Would expressing sympathy be enough? Probably not. So I took a deep breath and asked my former friend how much rent was due. "I'll send a check," I said. I made it clear that it was a gift.

After I hung up, I felt sorry for my former friend but strangely positive about myself. I had done a good deed. A few days later when I reflected back on that evening, I felt ashamed. My smug, self-congratulatory frame of mind struck me as rather ugly. Writing a check when you have money in the bank isn't really a virtuous act. It is more like painless charity rewarded with a feel-good ego boost.

In order to salve my conscience, I shared my misgivings with my friend Yvonne. She told me to stop beating myself up. "*C'est normal*," she remarked. "If all you felt comfortable about giving was money, that's fine. There's nothing wrong with feeling good about that." I welcomed her point of view, but I wasn't entirely convinced. A week later I recounted the same incidents to another friend, Michael. That conversation veered off in an unexpected direction though. Michael related how, when he hears a fire truck or ambulance go by, he turns in that direction, puts his hands together, and says a silent prayer of thanks. "They're bodhisattvas," Michael said. "They put the lives of others ahead of their own."

I had heard the term "bodhisattva" many times before, but I wasn't exactly sure what it meant. So I did a little research. A bodhisattva, I read, is anyone on the path to Buddhahood. We are all bodhisattvas, some sources said, whether or not we know it. I found this encouraging. If the impulse toward enlightenment is latent in all of us—no matter how unenlightened some of us may seem—this is surely hopeful news. I also read that at some defining point in a bodhisattva's spiritual evolution, they take a vow to delay their final enlightenment until every other sentient being is enlightened too. This, I assumed, is a metaphorical way of saying that enlightenment is a project of "we," not just "me." In other words, enlightenment involves extinguishing the notion that I am somehow separate or disconnected from all other sensing, feeling beings.

+ + +

If we are all bodhisattvas, then many of us are probably bodhisattvas in the manner of the protagonist of the motion picture *Groundhog Day* (1993). His name is Phil. Phil is an on-camera weatherman at a Pittsburgh television station. Egotistical, sarcastic, and insensitive to others, Phil is an unhappy man working at job he despises. As the movie unfolds, Phil and his crew travel to a small western Pennsylvania town to document an annual groundhog day celebration. If the groundhog (a small, hibernating rodent) sees its shadow when first emerging aboveground, then, according to the tradition, spring will arrive early that year. (If it is cloudy and there is no shadow, winter will persist longer.) After the broadcast, Phil and his crew learn that a huge impending snowstorm will oblige them to spend the night in this provincial outpost. Phil becomes even crankier. But then things turn strange. Waking up on what he thinks is the next morning, Phil finds that the previous day is simply repeating itself. And this daily repetition continues—over and over and over again—for what seems like years. Phil, however, is the only person aware of this ontological anomaly. At first he uses his foreknowledge to obtain what he thinks he wants from others. This becomes uninteresting. Then boring. Then depressing. Looking for a way out, Phil attempts suicide—only to wake up in the morning to face the same day yet again. Realizing that there is no possible escape, Phil begins to modify the way he looks at things. Slowly his character and personality change. He becomes genuinely friendly and kind. He finds enjoyment in helping others. He gets so immersed in "doing good" that he stops thinking about himself. And when his old self is completely forgotten, Phil, finally, wakes up to a brand new day.

The movie is, of course, a parable about what many of us have observed in our own lives. The same interpersonal conflicts, the same emotional blockages, the same bad habits and obsessions, the same resistances to change . . . keep reoccurring, in different guises, over and over and over again. In this regard we share much with Sisyphus. Yet, unlike Sisyphus, we can change the nature of our reality. We can transform our attitudes and modify our behavior. Like Phil, we are free to move on. To evolve.

+ + +

There is a weathered cement buddha, unperturbed by all the ugliness afoot in the world, sitting calmly on a terrace outside our family's dining room window. He is a symbol of wisdom and goodness, an optimistic reminder that enlightened, beautiful human beings can and do exist. Nevertheless, if you asked me exactly what "enlightenment" means, or if I've ever met an "enlightened" person, I couldn't say. There is someone who comes to mind though. His name is Guy. He was a dear friend. He was far from perfect but there was something extraordinary—beautiful—about the way he treated people.

Guy, like Siddhartha, was born into royalty, except in Guy's case it was of the Hollywood sort. His father was a famous songwriter. His family lived in a grand house surrounded by other grand houses where famous actors, movie directors, and celebrity singers lived. Contrary to the way it may have seemed, this was not an auspicious beginning. Most of the people I knew from similar backgrounds had painful struggles with life. Guy was an exception. Without direct family help, but with an incredible amount of what could be called luck, he experienced tremendous success as a photographer in the music and motion picture industries. Like Siddhartha though, when worldly success became distracting from what he perceived to be life's more important purposes, he put it aside. He moved far away from La-La Land and created a beautiful family.[39] I met him years later, after his return to California.

Guy was kind. There was a soft, joyful lilt to his voice. His manner was easy and relaxed. He was always positive and cheerful, no matter what the situation. If one of his prized motorcycles was destroyed, he would probably say something like, "What a shame. Oh well. At least nobody was hurt!" If somebody broke an arm and a leg, he would say, "Oh well. At least it wasn't both arms and legs!"

Guy knew a tremendous number of people. In his manner of speaking, everyone was his best friend. "So and So? Oh, he's my best friend." For a long time I thought this was hyperbole. How could one person possibly have so many best friends? However, whenever Guy interacted with someone, he made them feel as if they were the most important person in the world. At that moment they were, indeed, his best friend.

There was something else about Guy I found uncanny: He never squandered time. He always appeared to know exactly where he was and where he had to be next. I never saw or heard him discussing plans or schedules, but one to two hours seemed to be the limit of his attention in any one place. During these confined spans of time, I saw him dispense care, sympathy, love, tenderness, and other qualities of human concern. All of these interactions were interspersed with good humor and gentle laughter.

If I were to describe Guy in the epigrammatic manner he often used to describe others, I would say that he was the most profoundly superficial person I have ever met. I mean this as a statement of fact, not as a value judgment. If I had said this to Guy, he would have undoubtedly chuckled and replied, "That's a good one!" Guy seemed to glide over the unpleasantness of life, past all the petty disagreements, rivalries, jealousies, status mongering, and greed that surrounded him. He had no enemies. In other words, buddha-like, he never descended into the venalities or tragedies most people get drawn into. He skimmed along the surface. He did so with immense skill, and he did so right up until the very end.

In his later years, Guy had a couple of major health setbacks. There were medical procedures that could have possibly extended his life a little longer, but at a certain point he said that he had had enough. I phoned when I heard the news. He sounded as chipper and enthusiastic as ever. I tried to muffle my sobs, but perhaps he heard. In an upbeat voice he said, "I love you buddy. I've had a wonderful life. I'm not afraid." And then, as if everything was perfectly normal and natural he added, "Let's talk soon!"

That was Guy's last beautiful gift. Two days later he merged with the cosmos.

+ + +

It's easy to die.

Just give your breath

back to the trees

and the wind.

—Peter Levitt, from *One Hundred Butterflies* [38]

notes

1 The interviewer was Mariah Nielsen, an architect, design historian, and curator. We have since become friends.

2 This and nine other definitions of "aesthetics" and "the aesthetic" are published in the book *Which Aesthetics Do You Mean?: Ten Definitions* (Imperfect Publishing, 2010).

3 The title of the resulting book is *Arranging Things: A Rhetoric of Object Placement* (Stone Bridge Press, 2003).

4 The interior design of the flower shop, I later learned, was entirely reconfigured every Sunday. I must have passed by at a moment when the furniture was being moved around and all the flowers were in a back room.

5 *The Flower Shop: Charm, Grace, Beauty &*

Tenderness in a Commercial Context (Stone Bridge Press, 2005).

6 My mother and stepfather may have been inspired by the traditional Japanese method for preserving and finishing wood called *shou sugi ban* (or *yakisugi*). This process involves charring the wood with fire, which leaves a dense, carbonized layer of blackness. Supposedly it renders the wood waterproof and resistant to termites, fungus, and rot. Loathe to actually torch our house—which was located in a high fire-danger zone—they replicated this look with black paint.

7 The "spiritual authenticity" of my tea house became apparent to me much later when I looked back on it from the vantage point of having lived for many years in Japan.

8 This is what the mural depicted: As young Siddhartha leaves his comfortable family home in Beverly Hills, his mother and brother tearfully wave goodbye. • Arriving in Hollywood, Siddhartha becomes enmeshed in the amped-up worlds of marketing and commerce. He becomes obsessed with making money. • Siddhartha succumbs to the lures of sensual pleasure. • Weary of his "empty" life, Siddhartha hops on a motorcycle and heads up the Pacific Coast Highway. • Arriving at a boulder-strewn stream in an isolated canyon in the Malibu hills, Siddhartha sits down among the rocks and begins a prolonged period of meditation. • After achieving enlightenment, Siddhartha retires to a shack on a remote sandy beach and begins life anew as a portrait painter.

9 Some of my activities during those structureless months: I co-produced an outdoor film festival in a sand-filled lot near the ocean. It was called "The Venice Film Fricassee." • I opened a business called Eucalyptus Massage in a refurbished meat locker located in a former

supermarket on what is now called Abbot Kinney Boulevard. · I took a road trip (where there weren't any roads) to the tip of Baja California during the rainy season. · I was retained by a psychotherapist friend to model responsible adult-male behavior for a sensitive teenage boy. · I performed for the draft board. (At the conclusion of my performance I was deemed unfit for military service). · I spent a lot of time at the beach and in the surf.

10 It was an open-minded moment in the history of the UCLA graduate architectural school. I was especially fortunate to have first encountered Professor Eugene Kupper. He admired my Fine Arts Squad work and championed my entry into the school.

11 I stayed in school because of my mother. My mother was an important influence in my life as a role model, a moral authority, and a vigorous supporter of all of my artistic endeavors. Never

once did she ask me to do anything for her, except this one time: When I told her that I wasn't going to become an architect, her response was, "That's fine. But at least get your degree." I explained that a degree would have little meaning in my life, but she was insistent. It is true that my master's degree has been of no practical value, but I am very glad that I made my mother happy.

12 The process of gentrification in Venice didn't begin in earnest until well after I left for good in 1982.

13 In the Venice artist circles I was associated with, "pretty" was a pejorative term akin to "decorative." "Pretty" and "decorative" connoted a thin, surface beauty that lacked depth and resonance.

14 Some of the other studios in Venice and Santa Monica that I visited include those of

Charles Arnoldi, John Baldessari, Larry Bell, Vija Celmins, Ron Cooper, Guy Dill, Ned Evans, Fred Eversley, Sam Francis, Jim Ganzer, Robert Graham, Charles Christopher Hill, Allan McCollum, Ed Moses, Paula Sweet, James Turrell, DeWain Valentine, and William Wegman.

15 My most noteworthy bath-art pieces were probably: "17 Beautiful Men Taking a Shower," an accordion-style fold-out book (photographed in a stall shower set down in the middle of the living room of Paul Ruscha's Hollywood apartment). "23 Beautiful Women Taking a Bath," a silkscreen print (photographed in the imaginatively tiled sunken bathtub at Tom Wudl's Venice studio-living space). "Mud Bath," a lithographic print with a spray-painted overlay (photographed in, and using the mud from, the Brentwood backyard of art collectors Elyse and Stanley Grinstein). And "Pagan Baptism," a large-scale photographic print embellished with pencil drawing (photographed in the automotive grease pit—converted into a soaking trench—at Peter Alexander's Venice studio).

16 After many inquiries, I finally did track down the poster's creator. He was Bart Thrall, an artist I wasn't familiar with. Thrall later told me he had stapled a number of posters to utility poles in the Santa Monica, Venice, and Mar Vista areas.

17 For an overview and history of *WET*, see *Making WET: The Magazine of Gourmet Bathing* (Imperfect Publishing, 2012).

18 For the first year and a half of *WET*'s existence, I was its sole full-time employee. Thereafter *WET* went from being "me" to "we." At any given moment *WET* had at least six full-time employees. *WET* had a suite of offices on the second floor of a building located on the southwest corner of Windward and Pacific Avenues in Venice. For the last year of *WET*'s life, the

office was in a warehouse-like space in Ocean Park (Santa Monica), two blocks from the beach, across a narrow street from Bob Dylan's rehearsal studio.

19 The hotel was located in Harajuku, then a sleepy district of Tokyo. Shortly thereafter Harajuku became a hotbed of experimental youth fashion and eclectic merchandising. At the time there was only one hotel in the area. It was booked for me by a representative of the textile company that acquired the rights to produce sportswear with the *WET* logo in Japan.

20 I shut *WET* down primarily because I had learned about as much as I wanted to about running a magazine. The next phase would have been getting better at marketing, something I had no interest in. I probably could have sold the magazine name, but the thought of *WET* becoming a mediocre run-of-the-mill publication was too sad. I preferred retaining the memory of the magazine at its peak.

21 The name of the magazine was *Brutus*.

22 I was in my mid-thirties at the time.

23 I had previously wandered into a few Comme des Garçons boutiques in Tokyo. The merchandise was appealing and cleverly dis-played, and the interior design of the shops provocative. In other words, my curiosity level was high. The year was 1982.

24 The building, a gymnasium, was designed by Kenzo Tange, one of Japan's preeminent mid-twentieth-century architects. It was located in Yoyogi Park near the Harajuku train station.

25 While publishing *WET*, I was approached a number of times about making a book about the magazine. I wasn't interested then because

I was totally enamored with the notion of ephemerality. Books seemed much too permanent.

26 Overall, the book-making process was a joy. There was, however, one major learning moment that took me by surprise. As the book's author/designer, I was responsible for the text, images (both acquired and of my own making), and the book design—including the cover. Thinking like the creative director of *WET*, I put together a somewhat elaborate cover shooting with a model, stylist, and an assistant in a rented Tokyo studio. A lot of resources went into the shooting, but when the cover proof came back from the printer, something was wrong. I couldn't quite put my finger on it. The publisher seemed pleased with what they saw, but I still had doubts. I asked my friend Keiko, the editor-in-chief of Japan's largest circulation fashion magazine, out to lunch. Keiko's candor and directness was rare in Japanese society, which is why I

so highly valued her opinion. When I showed her the cover proof, she burst out laughing. "It's horrible!" she blurted out. My heart sank. But I knew she was right and thanked her profusely. At last I understood what was wrong: I had made a suitable magazine cover, but not something appropriate for a book. It was the unsubtle, in-your-face tone of the imagery. After considerable emotional drama, and with my editor's help, the publisher was persuaded that the cover had to be redone. We negotiated an agreement whereby the publisher's art director would come up with a new design and concept, but I had final approval. That worked for me.

27 The title of the book was *New Fashion Japan* (Kodansha International, 1984). There was also a French version (Herscher, 1984).

28 I was living in the guest room of my friend Taki Ono's home in the Shibuya district of Tokyo. The room had a Western-style bed.

29 My editor, Peter Goodman, started a company called Stone Bridge Press in Berkeley. We worked out a business arrangement whereby Peter handled the editing, the administration related to book distribution, and half of the promotion. I wrote and designed the book, supervised the printing, and figured out how to pay for everything. We published eight books this way. In 2008, I began my own company, Imperfect Publishing. Peter is still a copy editor of all my books.

30 The artist Maruo Suehiro drew in a lyrical style popular in early twentieth-century Japan. He was one of Japan's great manga artists in what I would call the "sex and violence" genre. By contrast my books were quite innocent; they are even appropriate for children.

31 The title of the book is *Wabi-Sabi: for Artists, Designers, Poets & Philosophers* (Stone Bridge Press, 1994; the current edition is pub-

lished by Imperfect Publishing, 2008). A follow-up volume titled *Wabi-Sabi: Further Thoughts* (Imperfect Publishing, 2015) further elucidates the wabi-sabi concept. (It also details the process that led to the making of the first book.)

32 At the time I was writing, designing, and publishing a bimonthly newsletter titled *Japan Design Close-Up*. It was my first and only experiment with the newsletter medium. The subscribers were mainly design-related companies in Europe and North America that wanted to keep up with the aesthetic and methodological currents running through Japanese design-related industries. Topics addressed in the newsletter included things like how intellectual property was regarded in Japan; how the design departments of large consumer electronics companies were organized and functioned; and how mass-produced frozen Japanese confections were designed. I published

the newsletter for about a year. I stopped publishing it when the underlying "selling more
stuff" agenda of the Japanese companies
became too dispiriting.

33 I spent a total of nine years in Japan spread
out over a period of approximately 20 years.

34 The title of the article was "In This Manhattan Apartment, Every Room Is a Testament to
Japanese Tradition," by Thessaly La Force. It
was published in the *New York Times T Magazine* on February 6, 2019.

35 I found it ironic that the chair had won a
number of "prestigious" design awards and was
included in the design collections of many
"respected" museums.

36 This was after my friend Peter Gutkin, an
artist and fine-furniture maker, had already
repaired the chair once. Every joint that Peter

didn't repair soon failed. So the chair actually went through two rounds of repairs—and still kept falling apart.

37 The article was titled "The Efficiency Dilemma," by David Owen. It appeared in the *New Yorker*'s December 20 & 27, 2010 issue.

38 This poem is from the volume *One Hundred Butterflies* (Blissful Monkey Press, 2011) by Peter Levitt. Used with the permission of the author (peterlevitt.com). I first found Peter Levitt's poems in the wonderful book *WHAT BOOK!?* edited by Gary Gach (Parallax Press, 1998).

39 Many years later Guy created another beautiful family also.